The FROG BOOK

Nature's Alarm

Sue Lawson
& Guy Holt

For my friend Trish 'Froggy' Foran
S.L.

First published in 2023 by

wdog.com.au
Melbourne, Australia

Designed by Guy Holt
Illustrations by Guy Holt

ISBN: 9781742036571 (hbk)
Printed and bound by Everbest Printing Co Ltd

10 9 8 7 6 5 4 3 2 1 23 24 25 26 27

Front cover Kurit Afshen, worldswildlifewonders; title page Kurit Afshen; p2 IrinaK; p4 Kurit Afshen, Michiel de Wit; p5 Kurit Afshen, PomInPerth; p6 Istimages, Vision Wildlife; p7 demamiel62, Ken Griffiths, Rudmer Zwerver, Valt Ahyppo; p8 Samuel Purdie; p9 Samuel Purdie; p10 Shutterstock, Victor Photo Stock; p11 Chros, Prachaya Roekdeethaweesab; p12 BlueRingMedia, Kurit Afshen; p13 Ken Griffiths; p14 Guy Holt, LifetimeStock; p15 EreborMountain, Maquiladora; p16 Douwe Schut; p17 Connie Pinson, Vladimir Wrangel; p18 Artur Tiutenko, Ken Griffiths; p19 davemhuntphotography, LMPark Photos, Rosa Jay; p20 Ken Griffiths, Trevor Charles Graham; p21 photowind, Steve Byland; p22 Ken Griffiths, skrcenyz; p23 Eric Isselee, Javi Roces; p24 Dirk Ercken, Ryan M. Bolton; p25 Dr Morley Read, Vampflack; p26 Kobby Dagan, Dr Morley Read; p27 Lauren Suryanata, Michiel de Wit; p28 tdoes; p29 Alexander Denisenko; p30 Guy Holt; p31 Kurit Afshen, Rattana, Savo Ilic; back cover Dirk Ercken, SKphotographer.

Thank you to Samuel Purdie.
WDB

A catalogue record for this book is available from the National Library of Australia

MIX
Paper from responsible sources
FSC® C124385

Contents

Introduction 4

What is a frog? 5

What's special about frogs? 12

Frog parts 14

Survival 18

Life cycle 22

Helping frogs 28

Make your own frog habitat 30

Glossary 32

Useful resources 32

Index 32

Introduction

What animal drinks and breathes through its skin, tastes with its eyes and can jump up to 30 times its length?

The frog.

Scientists believe frogs were alive when dinosaurs stomped across the earth. Frogs play a vital role in the environment and food chain. The health and survival of frogs depends on the health of their environment. That is why frogs are known as nature's alarm.

What is a frog?

Frogs are amphibians. The word amphibian comes from the Greek language. *Amphi* means both, and *bios* means life.

Amphibians are cold-blooded creatures that can live on land and in water. They belong to a group of animals called vertebrates, which means they have a backbone. Amphibians breathe with gills when they are young and with lungs when they are adults. Frogs, newts, toads, caecilians and salamanders are all amphibians.

There are more than 6000 frog species across the world. Frogs live on every continent except Antarctica, where it is too cold for them to survive.

Australia's frogs

The frog is Australia's only native amphibian. There are at least 241 frog species across the country. Of these, 21 new species have been identified in the last 10 years, so there could be more to discover.

Many species of frogs are found only in Australia. Since 1980, Australian frog numbers have been decreasing, with 43 species listed as endangered or vulnerable.

Australia has more than 240 frog species, but it has only one toad, *Rhinella marina*, better known as the Cane Toad. The Cane Toad is an introduced species.

The Australian Wood Frog, which lives in the tropics, can jump more than two metres in one leap.

Australia's Southern Corroboree Frog is critically endangered. This small poisonous frog lives in pools and bogs in the Kosciuszko National Park and is only active at night or on overcast days. The Corroboree Frog's bright colours warn other creatures that it is poisonous.

First Nations people and frogs

Frogs have always played an important role across First Nations' cultures. Frogs feature in many Dreaming stories. They are also an important messenger for Australia's First Nations people, showing them where to find water and signalling changes in seasons.

First Nations people know frogs are important in healthy ecosystems.

Some First Nations clans would dig up water-holding frogs during summer. They would squeeze water from the frogs before returning them to their underground homes.

New Zealand frogs

The name of native frogs in New Zealand is *pepeketua*. New Zealand has three surviving *pepeketua* species — Archey's Frog, Hamilton's Frog and Hochstetter's Frog. Frog experts had believed there were four species of frog but discovered the Maud Island Frog is the same species as Hamilton's Frog.

New Zealand frogs are unique. Like many other frogs, they are small, nocturnal camouflage experts. But they also have features that make them different from all other frogs.

New Zealand's frogs have no external eardrums. They also don't have vocal sacs, which means they can't croak. Instead, New Zealand frogs attract mates through smell and movement. Unlike other frog species, New Zealand frogs don't have tails. But they do have an extra vertebrae and tail-wagging muscles.

Hochstetter's Frog has more warts than New Zealand's other two frog species.

Archey's and Hamilton's frogs lay their eggs in damp places. The young develop inside the egg and hatch as frogs. The Hochstetter's Frog lays eggs that hatch as tadpoles.

New Zealand frogs were once widespread across the country's north and south islands, but now are found only in a few places.

There are three other frog species in New Zealand but they are not native to the country. New Zealand's other frogs are the Green and Golden Bell Frog, the Southern Bell Frog and the Brown Tree Frog. The three species are native to Australia and may have hitched a ride on a boat to New Zealand.

Hamilton's Frog is one of the world's most endangered frogs.

The Cane Toad

Toads are not frogs but they are amphibians. Australia and New Zealand do not have native toad species, but one toad does call Australia home. The Cane Toad, which is native to South and Central America, was introduced to Queensland in 1935 to kill beetles that ate sugar cane crops. These tough toads failed to control beetle numbers and quickly spread to become a pest. Authorities originally released 100 Cane Toads in Queensland. There are now more than 200 million in Australia.

Cane Toads lay up to 30,000 eggs twice a year. Cane Toad eggs are different from frogs' eggs. Frogs' eggs clump together. Cane Toads lay long strings of eggs.

Cane Toads have poisonous glands behind their shoulders. The glands secrete a toxin that can kill animals that eat the Cane Toad. This makes the Cane Toad a threat to mammals, reptiles and birds, including pets.

Today, Cane Toads are found in Queensland, the Northern Territory and parts of New South Wales. They continue to spread.

Is it a frog or a toad?

In most cases, it's easy to tell frogs from toads. However, some Australian frogs look like toads. There are ways you can tell the two apart.

Most frogs have smooth, wet skin and need to live near water. A frog away from water will die. Frogs have sharp faces and long legs that allow them to jump. Frogs lay clumps of eggs and these hatch into tadpoles.

Toads have dry and lumpy skin. A toad's lumps are sometimes called warts, but they are really glands that contain toxin. Toads have broader faces and bodies and shorter legs than frogs. Instead of jumping, toads crawl. Toads lay long strings of eggs and, like frogs, their young are called tadpoles. Toad tadpoles are usually black and rounder-looking than frog tadpoles.

A group of frogs is called an army. A group of toads is called a knot.

What's special about frogs?

Frogs have special features that help them find food, move and survive on land and in water. Every body part — from their skin to their long sticky tongue — has a special job.

Frogs also have amazing abilities that make them important to the food chain and the environment.

Food chain

The food chain shows how living things rely on each other for food and survival. Each plant or living creature has an important role in the food chain. Some species, such as lions and wolves, are predators. Others, such as rabbits and mice, are prey. Taking one creature out of the food chain disrupts the balance, causing animals and the environment to suffer.

Frogs play an important part in the food chain. They are both predators and prey. As predators, frogs eat insects, including flies and mosquitos, moths, dragonflies and grass hoppers. Larger frog species also eat worms, small snakes and even mice. Frogs help control the numbers of these species. Tadpoles keep waterways clean by eating algae and other plants.

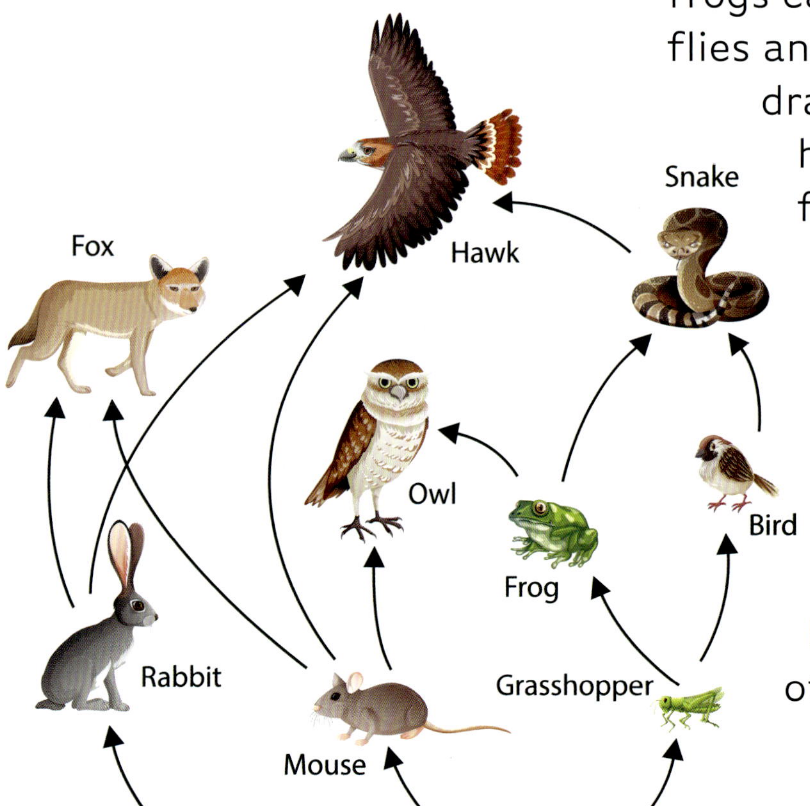

Frogs and tadpoles are also prey. Snakes, fish, birds and mammals such as foxes and cats eat frogs and tadpoles. If frogs became extinct, the number of flies, mosquitos and other insects would increase. Food would become scarce for snakes, birds and fish, which would threaten their survival.

Nature's alarm

Frogs play an important role in indicating the health of the environment. They are often the first creature to show changes in the environment. Frogs are like an alarm system. When frogs die or become ill, it can be a sign that their habitat is sick. Scientists call frogs bio-indicators.

Frogs are amphibious creatures, which means they can live on land and in water. Their thin skin is permeable.

Frogs shed their skin. Some species shed their skin once a week. Others shed their skin daily. Many frogs pull the old skin off their bodies and eat it.

Permeable skin allows water and air to pass through it. Frogs drink through their skin and also breathe through their skin, as well as through their nostrils.

But permeable skin has its problems. While it allows water and oxygen to pass into the frog, it also allows chemicals or pollution in the air and water to pass into their bodies. This makes frogs more at risk from pollution than many other species.

Frogs are also sensitive to changes in temperature or salinity in their environment. Scientists monitor frogs to measure health of the environment.

Frog parts

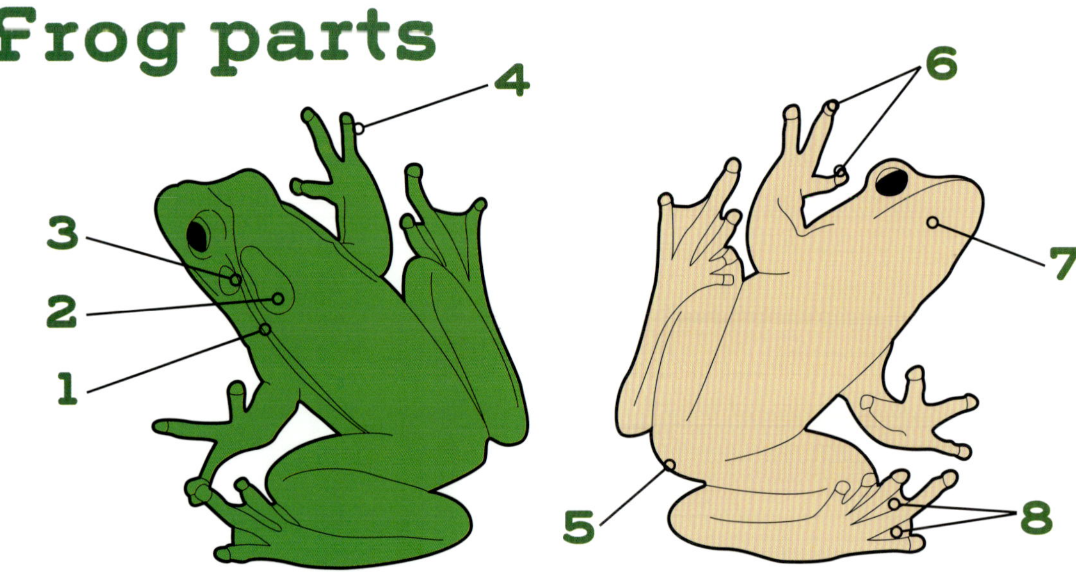

1. dorsolateral fold – ridge of skin separating the back from the side
2. parotoid gland – behind the ear and above the shoulder
3. tympanum – eardrum
4. fingers without webbing
5. cloaca – opening of the digestive, urinary and reproductive tracts
6. pads or discs – round, flat endings on fingers that help the frog climb
7. vocal sac – a sac under the throat which expands to make the male frog's call louder
8. webbed toes – their small front legs help them sit up on land

Move it

Most species of frog have long, muscular hind, or back, legs. Long hind legs allow frogs to jump or leap more than 20 times their body length. Frogs with long back legs are also good swimmers.

A few species of frog, like the Burrowing Frog, have shorter hind legs. These frogs can only hop short distances. They crawl or walk, like toads.

Frogs' small front legs help them to sit on land. The digits on a frog's front legs are called fingers and on the hind legs, toes.

Some frogs have webbed toes to help them swim, others, like tree frogs, have round pads on the end of their fingers and toes that help them to climb.

Sticky tongues

Frogs use their long sticky tongues to catch food. Frogs tongues are about a third of the length of their bodies and are covered in sticky saliva. This sticky saliva glues insects to frogs' tongues. Frogs shoot out their tongues, hit the insect and pull it back into their mouths.

Many frog breeds have small teeth, others have none. Frogs with teeth don't use them to chew, but to hold their prey still before swallowing. Once prey is in their mouths, frogs retract their eyes. Retracting their eyes helps frogs swallow their prey.

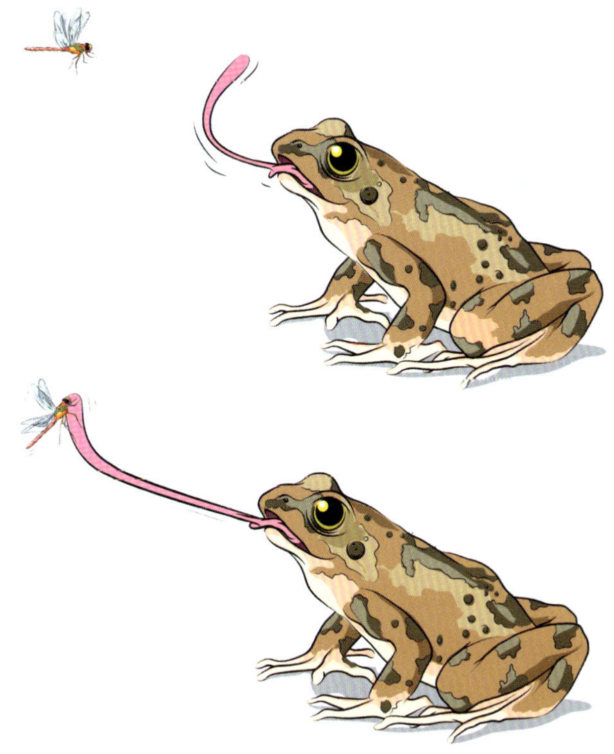

Frogs' tongues are attached to the roof of their mouth. This allows their tongues to reach out such a long way.

Seeing and swallowing

Frogs have large, bulging eyes on top of their heads. The position and shape of their eyes helps frogs see in different directions and when they are in the water. Frogs have excellent night vision too.

A frog's eyes have another important role. They help the frog swallow their food.

When a frog blinks, its eyeballs push down, creating a bulge in the roof of its mouth. This bulge squeezes the prey to the back of the throat to be swallowed.

Frogs taste food by touching it to their eye.

Nostrils and breathing

Frogs breathe through their nostrils and skin but can't breathe through their mouths. Frogs' nostrils, like their eyes, are on the top of their heads. This allows frogs to breathe while their bodies are under water.

To breathe through its skin, the frog's skin must remain wet. If the frog's skin dries out, it can't absorb oxygen.

The South American Waxy Monkey Tree Frog produces a thick waxy substance that it rubs over its skin to keep it from drying out.

Croaks and calls

Scientists believe frogs were the first land animals to have vocal cords. Each frog species has its own unique call. They make their call by filling the vocal sac under their mouth with air. The vocal sac also makes the sound louder. Some frog calls can be heard more than a kilometre away.

Only male frogs make sounds. During the breeding season they will croak to attract a mate. Female frogs are silent. Frogs are usually quiet during the cooler months.

Drinking

Unlike humans and other animals, frogs don't drink water. Frogs absorb water through skin patches under their belly and thighs. These patches are sometimes called drinking patches.

Survival

Frogs have been around for more than 200 million years. To survive this long, frogs have adapted to their environment. Their bulging eyes, permeable skin and webbed feet are all examples of adaptation. Frogs have also adapted to suit their habitat. Frogs live in many different habitats, from desert to rainforests. With such a wide variety of environments, frogs have developed amazing ways to survive.

The Australian Stuttering Frog, named because of its stuttering call, is also known as the Southern Barred Frog. Stuttering Frog tadpoles take up to 12 months to change into frogs.

Camouflage

Many frog species have specially marked skin that allows them to camouflage from predators. Frogs can sometimes look like leaves, be the same colour as leaf litter or blend in among rocks and logs. They will remain still so predators can't see them.

Vietnamese Mossy Frog

Grey Tree Frog

Poisonous

There are many poisonous frog breeds, especially in Central and South America. These frogs are usually brightly coloured — red, golden or blue. In nature, bright colours are often a warning to other animals.

Poisonous frogs secrete a toxin that sits on their skin. This toxin makes the frogs poisonous to touch. The Golden Poison Frog, also known as the Golden Dart Frog, is the most poisonous frog. This tiny species is less than a centimetre long and lives in the rainforests of South America. Just two micrograms of its poison can kill a person.

Rio Santiago Poison Dart Frog

Golden Poison Frog

Though frogs are many different colours, they can't see colour.

Ornate Burrowing Frog

Deserts and heat

Frogs that live in extreme conditions, like desert or arid areas, have developed unique ways to survive.

Burrowing frogs live in dry or arid areas of Australia. To survive the dry and extreme heat, these frogs burrow underground and stay there for months at a time. When it rains, the frogs emerge to breed.

While underground, several burrowing frog species continue to shed skin. The skin covers all of their body except their nostrils. This helps them conserve water.

Australian Crucifix Burrowing Frog

Frogs acquire a ring in their bones for every year they go into a state or torpor. The rings on frogs' bones are similar to how trees have a ring for each year of growth. Scientists can tell a frog's age at death by looking at the rings in its bones.

Ice and snow

Frogs, like all amphibians, are cold-blooded creatures. They rely on the weather to help them create body heat. In winter, many frog species become inactive. This is called a state of torpor. Torpor is similar to hibernation. Frogs that live on the land often stay above ground, but species that are good diggers will dig burrows for winter. Others bury themselves in mud at the bottom of waterways.

The Wood Frog, found in Northern America, can't dig. Instead, it spends winter in fallen logs, under leaves or in cracks in rocks. To survive, the Wood Frog stops its heart and other organs from working.

Frogs that live in these cold areas have a trick to stop them from freezing to death. Their blood has extra glucose, a type of sugar. This stops their blood from freezing. Once the snow and ice thaws, so too does the frog's body.

Wood Frog

Life cycle

Australia's frogs breed in spring and summer, when water and food are plentiful. However, if conditions are suitable in autumn, some species will also breed then.

Frog spawn

Most frogs lay eggs, or spawn, in dams, ponds, creeks and even puddles. The female frog lays the eggs, which the male fertilises. Female frogs can lay anywhere between 1000 to 2000 eggs a year, depending on the breed. Desert frogs may lay only 20 eggs each year. The Green Tree Frog can lay more than 10,000 eggs. Not all the eggs will hatch. Insects, dragonflies, water beetles and even fish eat frog eggs and tadpoles.

Frog eggs are surrounded by a clear, jelly-like substance. This clumps the black eggs together and helps them stay afloat. The jelly also sticks to plants to stop the spawn from being washed away.

Frog spawn can take three days to three weeks to hatch. The change from tadpole to frog takes longer.

Not all frogs lay eggs in the water. Many frog breeds in Australia and across the world, have adapted to lay eggs and care for young in ways that work with their habitat.

Metamorphosis

Frog eggs hatch into tadpoles. Tadpoles live entirely in the water and eat algae and other plants. They have gills and a tail like a fish. After approximately six weeks, tadpoles' gills disappear. They then breathe through lungs. Back legs grow first, followed by the front legs. At the same time, the tadpole's tail becomes smaller. While these changes occur, the tadpole's body changes shape. The tadpoles are now young frogs, sometimes called froglets, and will leave the water.

The process of a tadpole turning into a frog is called metamorphosis.

In America, tadpoles are called polliwogs.

Weird and wonderful

Frogs can be found in many different environments, including urban gardens, rainforests, swamps and deserts. To survive in these different conditions, frog species developed unique behaviours to suit them. Some of these adaptations are weird, but they are all wonderful.

The Central African Horror Frog can break its bones if threatened. The broken bones stick through skin and become claws for fighting.

The brightly coloured Poison Dart Frog in Central and South America lays its eggs on the rainforest floor. Both parents guard the eggs and keep them wet. When the eggs hatch, the parents carry the tadpoles on their backs to water.

The Asian Grey Treefrog builds a foam nest in trees above the water. The outside of the nest hardens and the foam inside keeps the eggs wet. When the eggs hatch, the tadpoles fall from the nest into the water below.

The female Darwin Frog, found in Chile and Argentina, lays its eggs on the rainforest floor. When the tadpoles start to wriggle inside the eggs, the male frog swallows them. The tadpoles develop in its vocal sac. The male frog spits them out when they are frogs.

The female Australian Pouched Frog lays eggs amongst the rocks and leaf litter in rainforests. After the eggs hatch, the male carries the white tadpoles in two pockets on its hips. Between two weeks and three months later, the young frogs emerge.

The Central and South American Marsupial Frog carries its eggs in a pouch on its back. After the female lays the eggs, the male fertilises them. It then moves the eggs to the pouch on the female's back. The eggs hatch as frogs.

The Glass Frog, found in Mexico, has transparent, or see-through, skin. When you look underneath the frog you can see its heart beating, stomach, liver and intestines.

The female frog may eat her eggs if she can't find enough food.

Frogs, like humans and other mammals, can drown if their lungs fill with water.

The Costa Rican Flying Tree Frog can spread its webbed feet to glide from branch to branch.

Frogs live in mainly freshwater habitats. However, the Leopard Frog from Florida can live in what is called brackish or briny water.

The Australian Gastric Brooding Frog had perhaps the most amazing breeding habits. The female Gastric Brooding Frog could turn off its stomach acid to brood its eggs in its stomach. The young frogs emerged from her mouth. The extinct species lived north of Brisbane.

A frog in captivity can live up to 20 years.

The world's biggest frog is found in West Africa. The Goliath Frog can grow to over 30 centimetres in length and can weigh about 7 kilograms. The smallest frog in the world is the Cuban Tree Frog, which grows to less than a centimetre long.

Helping frogs

After managing to survive for more than 250 million years, about one-third of the world's amphibians, including frogs, are threatened with extinction. In Australia, more than 40 frog species are listed as endangered or vulnerable.

The biggest threats to frog populations are loss of habitat, climate change, disease, pest animals and pollution.

Human activities like farming and housing have taken over frog habitats, leaving some species with nowhere to live. Chemicals and other pollution in the water and air pass through frogs' skin and can kill them. Introduced species like foxes, Cane Toads and cats catch and kill frogs. And rising temperature is reducing habitat and changing water temperature.

So, what can we do to help frogs?

There are simple things you can do. Take home your rubbish after a trip to the park or the beach, and be careful not to add anything to waterways. At home, watch what goes down the sink. Whatever goes down your sink will enter waterways and could make frogs ill or kill them. Talk to your family about chemicals. Ask them to stop using chemicals in the garden. Maybe you could make it a family project to find other ways to get rid of pests and weeds.

There's another simple and fun way you can help frogs. You can create a frog habitat in your backyard or at school.

Make your own frog habitat

You can create a home for frogs in your garden or at school. Talk to your family and to your teachers to see if this is a possibility.

Once you know it's okay to go ahead, there are a few things your frog pond or frog bog will need.

First of all, frogs need water, food and shelter to hide among. They also need the right amount of sun and shade. They need enough sun to help algae grow to feed tadpoles, but not too much or the frogs will overheat.

Once you have the right spot, it's then time to think about the pond. A frog habitat needs sloped sides so frogs can hop in and out of the water. A few rocks and logs in the water can help them climb onto land. You can use an old wading pool or even dig your habitat. If you dig out a place for frogs, line it with black plastic so the water doesn't seep away. Avoid using metal as frogs don't like metal.

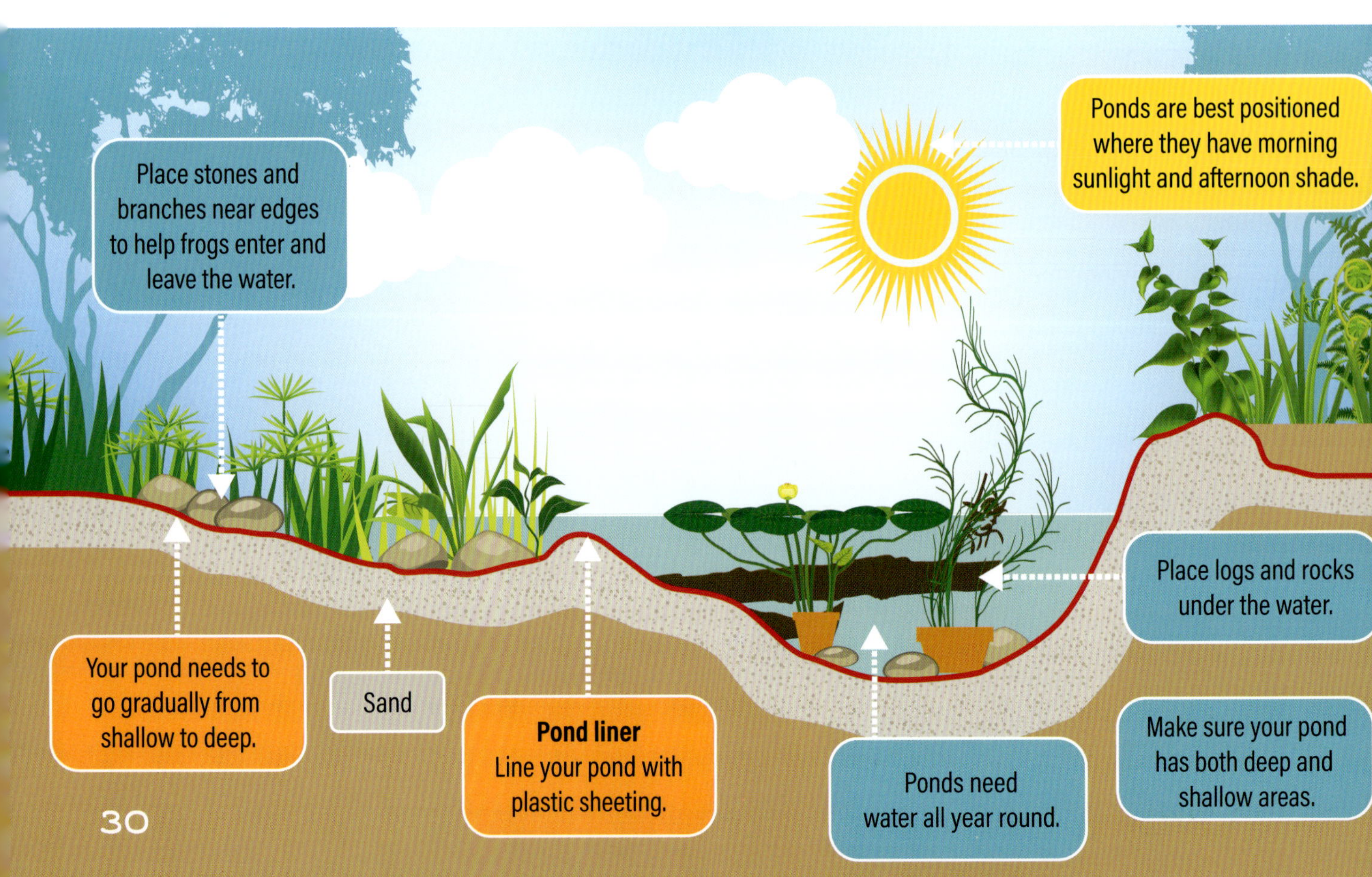

The final thing you need is water. Rainwater is best, as our drinking water has chemicals in it that frogs don't like. If you have a rainwater tank, fill the pond or bog. If not, allow the rain to fill it. Catch some extra in buckets.

Make sure your frog pond or frog bog is about half a metre deep. If the water is too shallow, it will become too warm for the frogs. There should be cover around the pond to provide shade. You can add logs, rocks or even old pipes for the frogs to hide in. If you like, you could add native plants. Talk to an expert about which plants are safe for frogs. Adding a solar light will attract mosquitoes, and other insects for the frogs to eat.

What's missing?

Frogs!

Once your frog habitat is created, there's no need to go searching for frogs to live there. Nearby frogs will come to it. Truly! Be patient and before you know it you will have a frog population croaking on spring nights.

Glossary

amphibian – a cold-blooded creature, such as frogs, toads, newts, salamanders and caecilians, which have young that have gills and develop into a lung-breathing adult

aquatic – lives in water

camouflage – how animals blend into their environment to hide

digits – fingers and toes

metamorphosis – process where a creature changes from one thing into another

permeable – material or skin that allows gas or liquid to pass through it

predator – an animal that hunts other creatures for food

prey – an animal that is hunted for food

spawn – name for frog eggs and the act of laying eggs

tadpole – frog larvae or young

torpor – an inactive state brought about by reduced heart rate and breathing and lowered temperature, similar to hibernation

vocal sac – a sac under the throat which expands to make the male frog's call louder

Useful resources

https://www.frogid.net.au

https://www.fats.org.au

https://www.frogresearch.com

https://australian.museum/learn/animals/frogs

https://frogs.org.au/groups

Index

anatomy 14-17
Archey's Frog 8-9
Asian Grey Tree Frog 25
Australia's frogs 6-7, 9, 11
breathing 16
Brown Tree Frog 7
camouflage 19
Cane Toad 6, 10
Central African Horror Frog 24
Central and South American Marsupial Frog 25
Costa Rican Flying Tree Frog 26
croaks 17
Crucifix Burrowing Frog 20
Darwin Frog 25
desert 22
drinking 17
eggs 9-10
endangered 9
First Nations people 7
food chain 10
Gastric Brooding Frog 27
Glass Frog 26
Golden Poison/Dart Frog 19
Goliath Frog 27
Green and Golden Bell Frog 9
Grey Tree Frog 25
habitat 30-31
Hamilton's Frog 8-9
Hochstetter's Frog 8-9
introduced species 6, 10, 28
Leopard Frog 27
life cycle 22
Maud Island Frog 8
Metamorphosis 23
nature's alarm 13
New Zealand frogs 8-9
poison 19
Poison Dart Frog 24
Pouched Frog 25
Rio Santiago Poison Dart Frog 18
seeing 16
snow 21
Southern Bell Frog 9
Southern Camouflage Frog 18
Southern Corroboree Frog 7
spawn 22
survival 18, 28
swallowing 16
tadpole 23
toads 6
tongue 15
torpor 21
vertebrates/vertebrae 5, 8
Vietnamese Mossy Frog 18
water 7, 11
Wood Frog 6, 21